THE WORLD AT WORK

People doing rare, traditional, or surprisingly common jobs you've never seen before

Michael Fuller

D1088094

Self-published with help from PrintNinja

Printed in PRC
First Edition
ISBN 978-0-9950164-0-8

PREFACE

Every photographer has a niche, a specialty, a particular area of interest. I purchased my first 'big' camera just weeks before my first 'big' trip. Ever since, my passions for photography and travel have been intertwined. Travel is my excuse for photography, and photography my excuse for travel.

Not surprisingly, I've long maintained that my niche is travel photography. But what the heck is 'travel photography' anyways? By its very nature, it's broad. Landscapes? Yes. Portraits? Surely. Nature? Of course. Street shooting? Certainly. Twenty-two buffalo at a funeral ceremony sacrificed with machetes? Sometimes.

I decided in 2014 that my life needed a little shake-up. Quitting my job; selling my belongings; becoming a vagabond – that sort of thing. I would focus on improving my writing and photography, and on completing one big project: a crowdfunded photography book. (Spoiler alert: you're holding said project in your hands). But what would be the book's theme? "Some Nice Photos from Mike's Travels" seemed pretty weak.

And so the question of my photographic specialty resurfaced. With a few ideas rattling in my head, I just began my trip. Months later I was standing on an impassable mountain road in Tajikistan. Closed for at least five more hours. No detour. So I got out and watched a ballet of labourers and equipment – dump trucks, tarmac heaters, and rollers – resurfacing the road. The mixed crew of Tajik and Chinese struggled to communicate, none of them speaking each other's language. It was fascinating to watch.

It was then that my thoroughly-bored friend keenly observed that I seemed particularly interested in learning about and documenting how other people work. That idea slowly solidified in my mind, like the cooling tarmac of the road.

Welcome to **THE WORLD AT WORK: People doing rare, traditional, or surprisingly common jobs you've never seen before.**

Michael Fuller
December 2015

RICE FARMER
China ◀ ▶

In southern China, some Zhuang people work amidst an exceptional landscape. The Zhuang constitute one of China's 55 ethnic minority groups.

The main industry around this village is rice farming. But here, the paddies don't just grow rice. They're also stocked with fish.

This brilliant practise of integrated farming is called 'agriculture-aquaculture'. But I just call it 'delicious'.

HUMAN SCARECROW
Indonesia ▲

Between torrential downpours, this man and his family run out from simple huts, swinging bamboo poles with plastic bags tied on the ends. In the weeks leading up to harvest, the family must repeat this constantly: the local birds are hungry, and love the taste of rice.

FLOATING ISLAND MOLLUSC FARMER
Vietnam ◀

In Halong Bay, artificial islands tethered to nearby limetone spires are home to unique people – and usually their entire families too.

Farming fish and growing molluscs, theirs is a water-world. These floating island people visit land only to purchase supplies or sell their catch.

FISHERMEN
Burma ▶

In northern Burma, the world's longest teakwood bridge spans Taungthaman Lake. Built in 1850, its 1200 scenic metres are mostly used by fishermen and by Buddhist monks travelling between the temple and a local university.

MUSHROOM PICKER
Haida Gwaii ◀

My body was aching. I just finished a two-day solo hike after two weeks without a bed. I remembered hearing about a hostel in the quiet logging town of Port Clements. (Population 440 – one of the area's largest towns)

I hitchhiked there, and when I walked inside I noticed one particularly young and dreadlocked dude. He was the last person I expected to be the owner.

Alan was an amazing young man: social worker, kayak guide, mushroom picker, world traveller, musician. His great hostel had hammocks, musical instruments, billiards, kayaks, sea views, and a great location.

He described his hostel's location thusly: "Grocery store downstairs; cafe across the street; pub on the corner. What more do you need?"

Drumming, discussion, and devouring delicious mushrooms for dinner (the ones pictured) was much more than I expected. All I wanted was a roof.

RICE FARMER / BULL RACER
Indonesia ◀ ▶

After rice harvesting ends, farmers in this region of Indonesia gather for a celebratory festival called the Pacu Jawi.

One rice paddy is selected, and transformed overnight into a festival ground. For just a single day over a thousand people gather to hear live music, ride home-made Ferris wheels, and watch bull races.

The animals sprint across the flooded field, followed by their owners: Either running (behind single cows), or standing on a plow (harnessed behind two bulls). They pull and sometimes even bite the bulls' tails — it makes them run faster.

DUCK-HERD
Burma ◀

The fishermen of Inle Lake practise a leg-rowing method seen nowhere else in the world.

It's believed that this 800-year-old tradition began because of the many hyacinths and reeds in the large, shallow lake. By standing, the fishermen can see further ahead and navigate around thick patches, while also handling their heavy nets.

FISHMONGERS
Zanzibar ▶

RIVERBOAT FOOD VENDORS
China ◀

The passenger ferries on the Yangtze River stop for only 3 minutes at each port. Ingenious food vendors still devised a way to serve these "drive through" customers.

To get a meal, you must shout your order from the boat. The vendors will then deliver the food and retrieve your payment simultaneously, with a fishing net.

STREET SNACK VENDORS
China ▶

In Beijing, the local delicacy is scorpions: Skewered live, ready to cook, in a variety of sizes.

When I originally shared this photo online, my friend from Beijing commented immediately.

"Those are only for tourists. Real Chinese eat McDonald's."

Below is an excerpt from one of my website's travel experiences. I wrote it during the nine weeks I spent exploring China:

Traveling through China with my friend Oker has provided an endless source of hilarity. Chinese-born but raised thoroughly-Canadian, he is an enigma to the local people, and for sheer delight he takes every opportunity to magnify their confusion.

For instance he dresses in somewhat ragged clothing, and wears a hat reserved for farmers. The locals suspect he's a poor rural peasant – an idea confirmed by his terrible Mandarin.

But then they notice something else: He's carrying a $3000 camera. And speaking English with us. But if he's a rich foreigner, why is he dressed in rags?

If that wasn't enough to confuse them, he's also illiterate. He often asks locals for help reading signs or menus. More than once they've responded with, "What are you, stupid?". To which he tells them, "No, I'm Canadian."

When asked outright by locals, he'll alternate between telling them he's our guide; we're his slaves; or that he's Japanese. The latter horrorifying to most rural Chinese.

SAMSA BAKER
Uzbekistan

CANE-SUGAR PRODUCERS
Indonesia ◀ ▶

At a simple shack in a Sumatran village, this family produces sugar from cane.

One man crushes the cane, extracting the juice, while his wife boils away the excess water in a row of bubbling cauldrons.

She fuels the fires with bamboo and a healthy sprinkling of plastic, a fuel sadly found in excess throughout the countryside.

When finished, the sugar is formed into round blocks. They look like hockey pucks, but taste better.

COOKS
China ▶

In a remote village we entered a restaurant and ordered a chicken dish. "You can't order just one chicken dish." they told us, "Because if we're going to kill a chicken for you, it makes two dishes."

"What?! – you're going to kill a chicken just for us!?" we asked, amazed. Now, they were confused. "Uh... how else do you expect to eat chicken?"

Their tone of 'any-more-dumb-questions?' required no translation.

DOUGH BOY
India ◀

FLOWER DEALERS
India ▲

The roti assembly line. The baker then takes a ball and expertly

Every day is a busy day in Kolkata's flower market. Most of these

As you enter the door your nostrils fill with an odour like sweaty socks. Welcome to the silk-reeling room. A woman stirs a steaming cauldron containing silk-worm cocoons by the hundreds. She slowly woman, who delicately wraps it around a wheel. Each individual cocoon's thread is almost imperceptibly fine, like spider's silk. It's hard to believe the resulting filament – still remarkably fine – is

TAILOR
Zambia

Earnestly hemming-away
inside "God's Mercy Tailors"

TYRE-SANDAL MAKER, Tanzania ◄

This man and the others in his neighbourhood (the tyre-sandal making area of town) are helping in a small way to solve a local problem, and inadvertently, a global one too.

These men provide some of the world's poorest people with cheap, durable footwear. But they also help solve a problem the rest of the world hasn't yet: How to recycle old tyres.

Though not everyone in Tanzania wears such shoes, among some groups like the famous Masaai of the Serengeti, you find no other footwear.

BLACKSMITH, India ▶

After the obligatory Taj Mahal visit essential to every tourist in India, I wandered through the backstreets of the surrounding city's old town.

Some of the friendliest people I ever met called out to me – one, asking sarcastically if I was lost. Another, asking if I felt scared being so far from other tourists. They were good fun, and all genuinely happy to see the rare tourist willing to walk off the extremely well-trod track in Agra.

This man's piercing aquamarine eyes and excellent beard caught my attention, and though he seemed unfriendly at first, he warmed as I took an interest in his work. Later, he proudly showed me his foreign-coin collection, a proud symbol of all the foreigners he's met over his life. And one especially befitting a blacksmith.

STEAM LOCOMOTIVE MECHANIC
India ◄

To reach Darjeeling you really ought to ride the Darjeeling Himalayan Railway. Its coal-powered "B-class" steam engines not only chug 78km along, and two vertical kilometers up, the mountain – they take you backwards in time, too.

The railway was built in 1881, and still uses many of the original locomotive engines. This loco is one of the newest. It was added in 1919.

FARRIER
Kyrgyzstan ►

Wandering through a weekly animal market I came upon a horse, tied up and strapped down like a lunatic. Surrounding it, all manner of tools fit for torture. What the heck was going on?!

I went over to see the men responsible and realised that in all my years on this planet I'd never before seen how horses get their shoes.

CONSTRUCTION WORKERS
Vietnam ◄

CIVIL WORKS CONTRACTORS
Indonesia ◀ ▶

On my final night in Sulawesi, my language skills were finally moving beyond the realm of "That please thanks." I spent an hour speaking with a crew of Javanese contractors – when they weren't hand-mixing cement, barefoot.

We made small-talk of our families; food; salaries (theirs, despite months away from their families, a humbling $200 per month), and the price of cigarettes. The latter so cheap in Indonesia that if they had to buy cigarettes at Australian prices, they'd spend their entire monthly salary in one week.

But the most astonishing part of our cultural exchange was this:

"Are you married?" they asked.
"No, but I have a girlfriend."

"Why isn't she here with you?"
"Because she doesn't have money to travel."

"Why don't you pay for her?"

When I finally explained the answer – namely, that her pride would not permit it – they stared, mouths agape in disbelief.

It was great to be reminded that the feeling of cultural bewilderment can run both ways.

CONSTRUCTION WORKERS
China ◀ ▶

Adjacent to the worksite on the left, I found a husband and wife working amongst piles of rubble. With dusty faces and calloused hands, they chipped hunks of cement off gnarled, rusty rebar. For each piece of liberated steel – perhaps five minutes' work – they would earn a few cents.

At the time, the city of Shanghai was undergoing a construction explosion. For a sense of scale, the amount of construction in one decade (to 2009) was equivalent to building, from scratch, the entirety of New York City.

And all this building wasn't happening in a vacuum. Residents of old neighbourhoods were being evicted en masse. In just one decade (to 2003) the government forcibly relocated over two million Shanghai residents.

These historic *lilong* neighbourhoods were demolished, thrown under the wheels of an unstoppable train: 'modern' China. And of course, 'modern' Chinese, which these workers were certainly not.

With all this in mind, I had a realisation: The rubble that the couple were recycling for mere dollars a day could quite possibly have been the remnants of their own, shattered neighbourhood.

BRICK MAKER
Zambia ◀

This man and his partner are contracted for a few weeks of work. They shovel out the clay from beneath an enormous termite mound and compact it into a brick mold. The earns $0.08 per brick, which they must share.

I spent four eye-opening months as a student working in a Zambian copper mine. I did a variety of work, including a one-week survey expedition into the wilderness, and teaching an introductory mining course to our surveyors. The white building in the background was my classroom.

My journal entries from that time are a barometer on my changing attitudes to culture, comfort, and normality. One entry:

"Today I visited the local grocery store to see if the rumours are true. They were.

Early each morning, a few enterprising customers buy up every loaf of bread, for $1 each. Then, with loaves piled high on a table in front of the store, they sell them, for $1.15.

Another group, trying to emulate this success, has now begun the same practice with toilet paper."

BRICK MAKER
China ▶

RITUAL SLAUGHTERERS
Indonesia ▲ ▶

At a Torajan funeral ceremony in Sulawesi, a man and a bull face off. Within one minute, the buffalo will be dead. Within thirty, it will be tidy pieces of beef. The slaughter of buffalo — this one, and many others — takes place on the third and final day of Torajan funerals.

During this particular ceremony, one-hundred pigs and twenty-four buffalo were killed. A 'medium sized' funeral. The meat is given to friends, relatives, guests, local charities, and as payment to these slaughterers-for-hire. None of it is wasted.

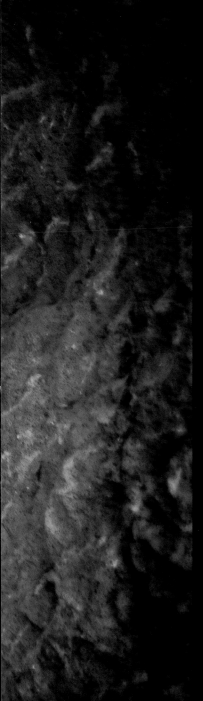

STONE-GRAVE DIGGER
Indonesia ◄

Outside a small village in Sulawesi, I peered up at a granite wall dotted with small wooden doors. A dozen sets of eyes peered back. Eyes of Tau-Tau, the carved wooden dolls that ward off evil spirits. And they guarded what lay behind all the small doors: Mummies. This was a vertical graveyard.

A single piece of giant bamboo, cut into a makeshift ladder, stretched ten metres skywards into an opening. Rock dust drifted out, along with the ringing of a chisel. Of course, I climbed up.

At the top I found this man chiselling tiny shards of eye-piercing rock everywhere.

In the unventilated cave, dust clung to his sweaty skin. He paused to chat, and told me that to cut one such grave it takes six weeks' work.

UNDERGROUND MINER
Chile ▶

In the world's largest underground mine, some operators complete their shifts without even getting their hands dirty.

This miner switches between cameras to monitor

oversized rocks, he will use remotely controlled hydraulic jackhammers to shatter the boulders.

Few mines, even in developed countries like Canada or Australia, are this technologically

STREET SWEEPER
Uzbekistan ◄

In Central Asia, I was amazed every day by the beauty and variety of people's faces. On this trip I quickly realised I needed to become a portrait photographer. Some faces looked as if they contained the entire world.

As was often the case in the region, this woman wouldn't agree to a portrait. Even with her face covered by a dust mask.

BUSKERS
Indonesia ◄

These boys serenaded patrons at a local noodle shop in Sulawesi's capital, Makassar.

PLASTIC RECYCLER
Indonesia ▶

On the city streets in West Sumatra, a child rifles through rubbish in search of plastic.

For every kilogram collected — no easy task, since most plastic bottles weigh under 20g — he told me he earns the equivalent of one dollar.

MINI-BUS DRIVER
Indonesia ▲

There isn't much asphalt on Flores Island, and almost all of it is contained on this, the 700km long Trans-Flores highway.

Private buses, outlandishly decorated (inside, and out) blare reggae music as they weave up mountain passes and down hairpin turns. Meanwhile, their passengers — many atop the roof — try to stave off motion sickness.

FERRY CAPTAIN
Indonesia ▶

Everyone makes mistakes. I'd boarded an overnight ferry during a national holiday. It was overcrowded, overloaded, and overwhelming.

To cope, I wandered around in my usual way: greeting everyone; talking to old ladies; playing guitar with teens; and making faces at babies. Then I noticed an open door: it was the bridge. After using my favourite question – "may I?" – the crew invited me in.

I nosed around and tried to stay out of their way, examining the charts and the navigational equipment. The second mate saw me and asked, "Do ferries in Canada have this same equipment?"

"I don't know," I told him. "Ferry crew in Canada don't let passengers wander around on their bridge."

He furrowed his brow, a mixture of confusion and perhaps disappointment at my backwards homeland.

Then I noticed one of his crew asleep on the couch in the corner. "Who's that?"

"The Captain," he told me.

"More like the Naptain," I chuckled to myself. Sometimes my hilarity cannot be translated.

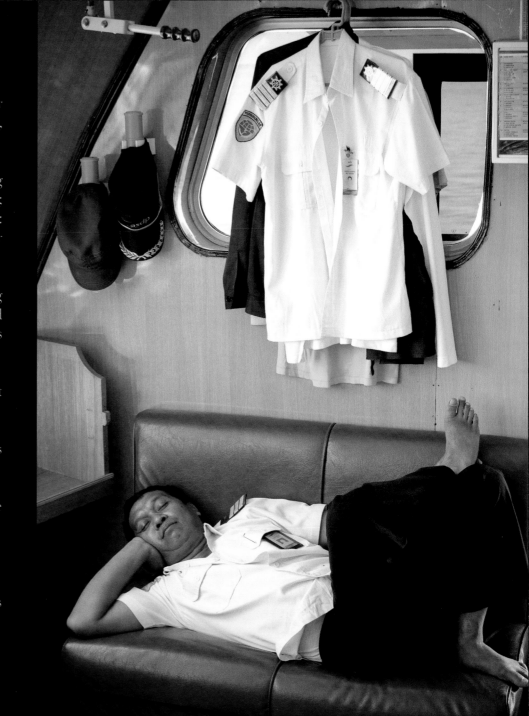

BOATMAN
Burma ▲

WOOD CARVER
Vietnam ▲

SHIPWRIGHTS
Zanzibar ▶

On the beach, with no shelter from the blazing equatorial sun, these men construct a traditional sailing vessel known as a dhow.

This design of sailboat has been used by Arab and East African traders on this coast for over 15 centuries.

SAND PAINTER
Senegal ◀

This artist in Senegal's capital uses eight different naturally-coloured sands, collected from across West Africa, and an adhesive from a baobab tree to create beautiful sand paintings.

HAT VENDOR
China ▶

Though we hiked along the less touristic area of the Great Wall, we still encountered vendors like this elderly man. He was selling communist hats without a hint of irony that, were his country truly communist, they would crush his enterprising spirit.

Irony was in high supply that day: We hiked with a young Mongolian surgeon working in Beijing. I mentioned to him how this Wall was actually built to keep Mongols out of China, yet here he was tramping all over it. Tragically, his English was too poor to understand my joke. I laughed enough for both of us.

MASAI CRAFT VENDOR
Tanzania ◀

BRACELET VENDOR
Peru ▶

"Would you like to buy a bracelet?" the man asked. I turned my head and let out a little gasp. His face had more piercings than a porcupine's mattress.

"No thanks," I said. My wrist was sufficiently braceleted.

"Well," he said, not so easily swayed, "What if it came with… a little gift?"

Being in Bolivia's capital, La Paz, we knew what kind of gift he meant. The powdery white kind derived from the coca plant.

"OK," I said. He'd convinced me.

"I'll buy one bracelet. But instead of that gift, let me take your photo."

BAR WRANGLER
Laos ◀

Fifteen years ago, Vang Vieng was a quiet riverside town surrounded by stunning karst peaks on the dusty, rough, and winding road between two of Laos' major destinations.

A quirky old Lao man named "Mr T" had an organic mulberry farm a few kilometres outside of town, where travellers would stay and volunteer milking goats, picking mulberries, and teaching English in local villages.

One day Mr T patched up some old tractor inner tubes and sent his volunteers on a relaxing float down the river. He could never have imagined the beast his idea would become.

Ten years later, the town had transformed into what Lonely Planet described as "an atmosphere of lethargy by day and debauchery by night". This culture revolved around river tubing.

The riverside bars employed a unique crew, who'd torpedo plastic bottles to potential patrons with practised precision. The wranglers reel them in to where the thumping music, drinking games, and drug-fuelled partying starts at noon and lasts until sundown. Right beside Mr T's once-tranquil organic mulberry farm.

CIGAR ROLLER
Burma ▶

FIRE SPINNERS
Thailand ◀

Every night on the tropical island of Ko Tao, this trio of talented teens would spin fire at a popular beach bar. They were the best I'd ever seen. They'd been practising daily for years.

I learned after the show that they were not from Thailand, but economic migrants from Burma. And despite their incredible skill, they weren't paid by this bar. These boys' only income came from tips.

The fate of their stomachs, and their futures, depended on the kindness of the too-often drunk and distracted young backpackers who frequented this bar.

ACKNOWLEDGEMENTS

My first thanks goes to all the subjects in this book, who sadly will never know how I've tried to show people the world through them. Like thousands of other strangers I've met in my travels, many of the subjects in this book reaffirmed my belief that humans everywhere are generous and caring. Thank you for allowing me to take your photograph, and keep a piece of you in my mind and heart forever.

This was a crowdfunded project, and I am enormously thankful to all my generous contributors. If just one of you hadn't helped before the deadline, this book could not and would not have been made. You know who you are – but just in case, I've listed all your names here.

Many others helped too, whether by offering a roof while I was travelling and working on this book; brainstorming the crowdfunding campaign; answering endless design questions; or all three (that's you, Tiff Shen).

I send my final thanks to everyone who has enjoyed my work – whether on my website; my Facebook page; or my mailing list. Your encouragement helps me to continue telling stories and sharing photographs from the lesser-known corners of this amazing world we all call home.

CROWDFUNDING CONTRIBUTORS
(in chronological order)

Jessica Berry
Cal Sandford
Nick Hain
Jon Fuller
Jeffrey Costain
Richard LeRoy
Lucy Ridsdale
Globes/Hillel Koren
Deborah Hewton
Louise O'Rourke
Alex Thomson
Susie Kaye
Lynn Martel
Jennifer Williams
Jennifer O'Rourke
Laurence Shapiro

Harold Albrecht
Marion McCleary
Steve Hart
Rob Rouwette
Susan Welstead
Val Greenfield
Thelma Bromley
Stephen Allport
Samantha Hille
Kara Serenius
Sheena Choy
Jacqueline Tam
Andrew Raymer
Erika Delemarre
Mi-chi Huang
Julia Fuller

Louis Kent
Gareth Llewellin
Janine & Paul Daniels
Rowan Gallagher
Jon Purdy
Gerd Gaberdan
Chris Hillier
Bev Hurst
Michael Fletcher
Megan Cosby
Jamie Ally
Samantha Hille
Hannah Moal
John Breed
Jackie Hallet
Trudy Worthington

Brent Patton
Kate Bailey
Kathy Sinclair
John Sinnott
Stephen Allport
Chris Hess
Qing Liu
Wayne Purcell
Paul Niven

Thanks again to you all, and also to those who couldn't contribute but helped by sharing my crowdfunding campaign.